Discover Your Personality!

When You're Unsure About Your Myers-Briggs® Results

---

by
Brian Jones

Table of Contents

Introduction

Have you taken the Myers-Briggs Type Indicator© or MBTI© one or more times, but are still not sure what type you are? Then this book is for you. Perhaps you're one of those people who just can't decide if they prefer Judging or Perceiving. Again, this book is for you.

This is a collection of insights about personality types gathered from years of talking to thousands of people about their MBTI results, conversations in which many have told me how they go about their daily lives, what they like and what they don't like.

I've sorted these anecdotes into groups to help you decide what describes you better. If you read about what the Perceiving and Judging types like to do, you should be able to see if one group or the other group is a better fit. If you are one of the undecided people, you might find yourself agreeing with six actions for the Perceiving types and five habits of the Judging types. That's okay. We're trying to see if one group fits better, but there's a good chance no single style will exclusively describe you.

Generally, books have descriptions of the different personality types. There are none here. My thought is that reading about the description of a type is best when you're sure which type you prefer. And if you can't decide .. . that's where this book comes in. Its purpose is to help you determine which side of the four scales you prefer.

Likewise, you will not find a discussion of what the four scales on the MBTI mean. I assume you already have some basic knowledge of the instrument and I did not want to repeat what many others have written before. I also assume you have already taken the MBTI and know what your results were. If not, you can do that on my website at http://www.discoveryourpersonality.com/

You should know the genuine Myers-Briggs costs money to take. If you took a free test or one that cost $10, it wasn't the real MBTI. There are many imitations out there, which is another reason the results can be off. Frequently, the free or really inexpensive tests are not as accurate as the real deal.

Finally, this book is for those who are interested in personality types, and would like to hear what others say about their preferences. I've experienced this countless times: I'll be explaining something that Intuitive types commonly do, and the person on the phone will start laughing, realizing she's not the only person who does that. I'm passing along the things people say about their types so you can take advantage of my experience.

The Difference Between Anecdotes and Research, and Why That Matters

It's important to note that this book is not based on research. I'm not sure research would help you decide which side of the scales you prefer. Here's why:

Whenever you read a study about some personality issue, the results frequently state something like: "75% of Extraverts like going to parties." Okay, does that mean you should or must like going to parties if you're an Extravert? No. If you don't like parties, can you still be an Extravert? Sure. Does it mean you cannot like parties if you're an Introvert? Also no. It may seem obvious that Extraverts like parties and Introverts don't, but being obvious and being accurate are not the same thing.

The information I'm presenting in this book is based on what's called anecdotal evidence, which is defined as "referring to the use of particular instances or concrete examples to support a general claim." It's not scientific and wouldn't stand up in a court of law.[1] I've used 'concrete examples' gathered from thousands of people, but it must be kept in mind that the plural of anecdote is not data. Even with all the people I have spoken to, it's important to remember this is not the same as research. Research requires a lot of preparation, a valid sample, statistics, good analysis and other people who can check your work for accuracy and completeness before you can draw any conclusions.

Here's my standard disclaimer:

---

1   http://grammar.about.com/od/ab/g/anecdoteterm.htm

None of what I've written here is to be confused with science.

These are the results of my talking to thousands of people over the years.

Statistics describe groups, not randomly selected individuals from those groups. People often think that all statistics about any group they belong to must apply to them. Not true. For example, if we say most engineers are Thinking types, it does not mean you cannot be an engineer if you are a Feeling type, or that you *must* be an engineer if you are a Thinking type. Even if we say that 90% of engineers are Thinking types,[2] it's not an indication of what *you* should do. It would still mean 10% of engineers prefer Feeling. Let's say 80% of people do not smoke.[3] Are you a smoker? There's no way to know by looking at statistics. If we put a group of 1,000 randomly selected people in a football stadium, we could accurately predict 80% do not smoke. What if you're in that group? Again, there's no way the statistics can show if you are a smoker or not, and it doesn't change the statistics, or their predictive value.

Your Experiences Don't Matter When We Talk About Groups.

It's important to remember your personal experience is meaningless when describing groups. By definition, each

---

2   I have no idea what the actual number is; it's just an example to illustrate the point.

3   Likewise

of us has limited experience because we have only one life. When we read statistics like "70% of smokers get some form of cancer,"[4] invariably, someone will say something like, "My Uncle Bob smoked three packs a day for 80 years and he was never sick a day in his life. He died at age 90 from falling down the stairs." The implication here is that the statistics are wrong but no . . . the statistics are correct. You did not see all the smokers who died at 40, 50, or 60, so you have no basis for comparison. You're thinking about your Uncle Bob. But out of 1,000 three-pack-a-day smokers, how many live to 90? I'd guess very few. You do not have access to those facts, but researchers do. Yes, it's true; some smokers will live to a very old age, but not many. It's far more likely they will die much younger than that. So when you read something that does not agree with your personal experience, consider the possibility that your experiences are not the norm. (Yes, Judging types, I am talking to you.) The statistics could be accurate, even if they conflict with your personal experience, like my Uncle Bob example above.

There is something called a "sample of convenience." This means it's not a random group formed from all people, but instead is composed of individuals who fit certain criteria. In this case, the people with whom I speak are generally looking for some kind of answer or insights, which makes them part of a self-selected group and not a random sample. People who are completely satisfied and fulfilled in their careers are probably not going to talk to me about their futures, so we cannot draw universal conclusions from

---

4   Likewise

this sub-group. This is also true when you see things like personality type tables for Mexican managers. That is not a random sample of all Mexicans, but a select sub-group of managers. We cannot draw conclusions about the entire population of Mexico based on results from the manager group; we would have to compare managers from different countries to see how similar or different they are.

I'm going to use shorthand in this book. For example, the correct way to refer to a "Thinker" is "someone who has a preference for Thinking." Unfortunately, that is a clumsy way to write a book, so when you read "Thinker," remember to fill in the blank with the long version.

When I talk to people on the phone, the style and direction of the conversation are determined by the person with whom I'm speaking. When putting this into book form, I used all the different things I say to the various personality types. This means you will likely read things you won't like or perhaps will find insulting. In a real conversation with your type, I wouldn't say those things. It would be impractical to write 16 different books, so it's all here. Some people need and appreciate a kick in the pants. Others need more hand-holding and empathy. There's no way to know what would be best for you, the reader, so look for the parts that speak to you and try to overlook the rest.

Many of the examples I use in this book are directed at those who live in North America. When I speak to people from other countries, I use other examples, the metric system, and less colloquial speech. If you are one of those people, I ask for you to understand my reasons for structuring this book for North Americans. While our conversation would be different if we were speaking on the phone, incorporating all of those issues within one book was just too complex.

The Most Common Misconception About the Myers-Briggs Type Indicator©

The MBTI does not measure quantity, so your score on the Clarity of Reported Preferences does not show how much of an Introvert or Extravert you are and, in fact, there's no such thing as a "slight" Extravert or a "strong" Thinker or an "extreme" Judger. The MBTI shows preferences, not degrees. When the scores are slight or the bar graph is near the center line, it does not indicate you are balanced between the two; it usually means you're not sure which side you prefer. One person asked me if the "best" profile would be every scale at the center line, indicating, in his opinion, a completely balanced person. My answer was "no" . . . that would probably be a person who was totally confused about everything.

Remember, the MBTI is about dichotomies – mutually exclusive states, such as on/off, dead/alive, wet/dry, or tall/

short. A light switch cannot be both on and off. A fish cannot be both alive and dead. What we're trying to do here is find out which side of each scale is easier for you to use, which you prefer. Yes, you likely do both Sensing and Intuitive activities every day, but which comes more naturally to you?

What this means is there is no difference between 12, 19, and 28 on a scale. Like our light switch, it's either on or off. All three scores show someone who probably prefers extraversion, for example. People will say things like this: "The last time I took the MBTI, I got a 25 on extraversion and this time, I got a 12, so I was more extraverted in the past." This is not how it works. Like our light switch, it's either on or off, yes or no . . . either you prefer extraversion or you don't.

As the scores move closer to 1, the likelihood you're not sure about which side you prefer increases. So a person with a score of 30 on Judging likely will be very clear about her preference for that side of the scale. The person with a Clarity Index of 1 is very possibly unsure about which side he likes better. That is something we would explore in a conversation.

It's common for people to say things like, "At work, I'm a Thinker and I'm a Feeler at home." A better way to think about it might be to note that you must do many Thinking-type tasks at work, so you have become quite competent at using that side of the scale, but you probably prefer Feeling. For most people, the way you act at home is more likely to be a true representation of your preferences than what you have learned to do at work.

Why? Because work (or school) often requires us to modify our behavior to fit in, get along, and be successful. Behavior is not the same as personality. You can choose, start, stop or modify behavior, but you don't get to choose your personality, just as you don't get to choose whether you're right- or left-handed.

Here's an example: most people yell more at their families than at their boss, colleagues, or customers. If you start yelling at your colleagues and/or your customers, very quickly you and your boss will have a discussion. If you continue to yell at your customers, you will probably lose your job. However, if you continue to yell at your family, they will still be your family. They may not like you or want to spend time with you, but they can't fire you. Many people are on their best behavior at work and their not-so-best behavior at home. For that reason, the way you behave at home is more likely to be accurate than how you have learned to, or are required to, behave at work.

In this book, you will read why, many times, it's better for you think about how you behave at home, not at work or school. The reason is people struggle to separate the two. I've experienced this hundreds of times: I will tell someone to think about how they behave at home, and the *first thing* they say is, "Well, at work I . . ." The reason is that work dominates our lives so much, people tend to automatically go into "work mode" when talking about behavior. Therefore, it cannot be said often enough, in my experience. I know you'll get tired of reading it, but it's there for a good reason.

Explaining the MBTI© in 90 Seconds

Get a piece of paper and something to write with. Then sign your name and write the numbers 1,2,3,4, and 5 on the paper. Next, put the pen or pencil in your opposite hand and repeat.

What most people report is that it's significantly easier to do this exercise with their dominant hand. Yes, you can do it both ways, but one way is usually much easier than the other. Using your non-dominant hand often takes much more time, effort, and concentration and the results are usually larger, sloppier, and look like they were written by a small child.

The same is true with personalities. Now, you likely do both extraverted and introverted tasks all the time, just as you use both hands every day. However, skilled activities such as writing, using a pair of scissors, or threading a needle will be easier for most people if they use their dominant hand.

In the same way, if you prefer Extraversion, you will probably feel worn out if you have to do a lot of introverted activities and vice versa. If you have a job that requires many Sensing activities and you prefer Intuition, you will likely find that job to be tiring and to require a lot of effort on your part. Sure, you can do it, and you might even become quite skilled at it, but that's not the same as being your natural preference.

The idea here is that the more things you do that are in alignment with your preferences, the easier they will go. Of course, that does not mean you'll have zero problems or everything will always go your way. On the contrary, life rarely works out that way. This is why we have the saying, "Man plans, and God laughs." Still, if you're a right-handed person, using your right hand to cut paper with scissors is going to be a lot faster, smoother, and take less mental energy than doing the same task with your left hand. Likewise, if you are a Feeler type, you're probably going to like those jobs in which the Feeling style is valued, accepted and appreciated a lot more than jobs that require Thinking-style skills. Therefore, if you have to work at something, force yourself to do something or concentrate hard to do something, it's probably not your natural style. Instead, it's probably something you've learned how to do.

When we talk about preferences and hands, there's another idea to consider: there's no rule or law that says you have to be either right- or left-handed. You can be both; you can be neither. The same is true with personality types. There's no rule that says you must be either a Thinker or a Feeler, for example. It's perfectly acceptable to be undecided on any scale you choose. Some people use the letter "x" in that case, and describe themselves as an ISxJ, for example (**I**ntrovert, **S**ensing, **U**ndecided, and **J**udging). If you think that's the best description for you, then that's the answer. In my experience, I would guess about 15% of people come to that conclusion on one or more scales, something that seems to be more common among Perceiving types.

It's also the case that many of us will use different sides of the scales as required, just like we use our hands. For example, if you're a right-handed person, talking with a telephone in your right hand and you want to write something down, many times you will automatically switch the phone to your left hand so you can continue to talk while you write with the right hand. You did not suddenly become left-handed; you're using your left hand in this situation because you need it.

The same is true with personality: if you have to work on a math problem, you will likely use the Thinking style, regardless of your preference. To console someone who has lost a loved one, most of us will use the Feeling style, regardless of our preference. We switch back and forth as required by the situation, but we still probably prefer one style over the other.

How to Decide if You're an Extravert (E) or an Introvert (I)

?

You will now read about some common situations and how Extraverts (E) and Introverts (I) react. The idea is to give you a number of examples describing different behavior. You will want to see if you agree more with one side of the scale or the other. I've noticed that people will often agree with some parts of both styles. That's fine. We are trying to see if one style fits better. Remember, that's probably going to be the way you behave at home, and not at work or school. If you've learned how to do something or have to force yourself to do something, it's probably not your natural preference.

Okay, so what are the differences between Extraverts (E) and Introverts (I)?

This is the scale many people think they understand; they believe Introverts are quiet and shy while Extraverts are the talkers. Yes, that can be true but it might also happen that, if we're discussing something she's interested in, an Introvert will talk your ear off.

Some say that Extraverts are more energized by the outer world, while Introverts are more energized by their inner world. Or that Extraverts have an outer focus and Introverts have an inner focus. Yes, you can think of it that way, but you'll probably want to read about concrete examples to see what that means.

Here are a few scenarios for you; as you read them, think about what you would do:

Being the Center of Attention in an Uncontrolled Situation:

Let's say you are at a large dinner party, with 60 people in the room. Suddenly, without any warning, someone across the room asks you to stand up and tell a joke. What would you do? Many extraverted types would get up and tell a joke, smile and wave at the group and enjoy the attention for a minute or so. In contrast, many introverted types would refuse; they have not prepared a joke and they don't want to look foolish or embarrass themselves, so they will simply refuse to stand up.

What I described above is an example of being thrust into the center of attention in an uncontrolled situation. Many extraverted types can easily handle such events, while many introverted types avoid them if they can, preferring to maintain control if it's possible. For example, an Introvert explained how she never answers the phone in her office when it rings. She always lets the call go to voicemail, then listens to the message. She looks in her files for notes or information about the customer who called, then calls him right back. She does this because she does not like to be surprised by telephone calls. She prefers to listen to the message, prepare her answer and then contact the customer.

Let's contrast that with being the center of attention in a controlled situation. One example is being an actor in a play. The audience is watching. You have memorized your lines. You have thoroughly rehearsed your role. The other actors are going to perform known actions and say known words. It will follow a plan. There will be no interruptions. There will probably be no surprises. You are pretending to be a character in a play while the real you is hidden safely inside.

It's the same with a teacher in a classroom. You can prepare your lesson plan in advance, think about which activities you'd like to do with the class, and mentally rehearse what you will do and say. When the class starts, you are in control. You are the authority figure. You might be standing while the students are sitting, which puts you in the power position.

Another controlled situation would be if you were asked to give a speech about some work-related topic at a conference. You will have time to prepare your speech and make notes in advance. You can practice at home. You will speak about a familiar subject to people who will listen attentively and are not likely to interrupt. You might be standing behind a lectern to shield you from the audience's view. If they ask questions, they will be about your material or subject. You can feel in control the entire time. That's something many introverted types can do well and even enjoy. It's not the same thing as working the room at a cocktail party where everyone's a stranger to whom you're supposed to be charming and witty. Many introverted types would rather not do that.

How You React to Surprising News:

The second example I use to show the difference between the introverted and the extraverted style is how they react to sudden, dramatic news. Without any kind of warning or hint that something is coming, with no inkling something is wrong, what happens if their partner says: "Honey, we're getting a divorce"?

Many extraverted types will start talking immediately, asking questions like, "What's going on? Do you have a girlfriend? Have you been cheating on me? How long have you been thinking about this?" and similar questions. In contrast, many introverted types might think these thoughts, but they have to process them internally before they can speak. It might take them 15 seconds, 15 minutes, 15 days, 15 weeks, or 15 months, but they usually have to run the information through their brains before they start asking the questions.

When Introverts react that way, they can be falsely accused of not caring. Extraverted types will say something like this: "I told her we're getting divorced, and she just sat there." Yes, it might look that way on the outside, but inside, everything is in turmoil. In a similar fashion, introverted types are sometimes praised for remaining calm in a crisis. Again, externally, it might look that way, but inside, it can be chaos.

Being Around People You Don't Know:

A third example is spending time with a large group of strangers, such as at a festival, concert, or busy shopping center. Many extraverted types find that exciting or energizing. They may talk faster or louder. They might stay up late or all night, because they get energy from the group. An Extravert said she purposely waits until the shopping center is full to go shopping because otherwise, it's just too boring.

It's quite different for many introverted types. Large groups of strangers often wear them out very quickly. An introverted woman told me she prefers to go shopping Monday morning at 10 a.m., when the stores are the least full and she can get in and out as quickly as possible. For many introverted people, online shopping is one of the greatest inventions of all time.

Can you say which of the two styles fits you better yet? If not, read on:

What would you rather do: spend three weeks alone in a room with just books, and no Internet, TV, computer, or telephone, or spend three weeks on a tour bus with 30 non-stop talkers for 14 hours every day? As you may imagine, more Introverts would choose the first option.

Expressing Emotions:

Many of us know people who are on their cell phones many times a day to tell their boy- or girlfriends things like,

"I miss you too, sweetheart. I can't wait to see you tonight. I love you so much. You are the sunshine of my life," and make kissing sounds into the phone. Many extraverted types can find that charming, cute, romantic or an indication that the person is madly in love. Many introverted types think, "If you have to say 'I love you' 25 times every day, something's wrong." The old Introvert joke goes like this: "I told you I loved you when we got married. If something changes, I'll let you know." An introverted woman told me, "I tell my husband I love him once a year on his birthday." I think she was joking, but maybe not.

OK, here are several additional scenarios for you. Think about how you would react in these situations:

Having People Look at You:

An introverted woman described how in a restaurant, she does not like walking across the room to go to the restroom, because she does not like people looking at her. She would rather walk along the outside walls or in some other way so that she is not noticed rather than walk through the middle of the room where everyone can see her.

Interrupting Others:

Many Introverts agree with the statement, "You have two ears and one mouth. You should use them proportionately." Extraverted types are more likely to interrupt another person who is speaking. It's not because they are rude; it's because they want to participate in the discussion and they're excited about sharing what they think or feel. Introverted types are more likely to wait for a pause in the conversation before speaking but, unfortunately, if they are with a group of Extraverts, that opportunity may never come.

Focus and Concentration:

An Introvert described how he missed a flight at the airport. He was sitting at the gate, waiting for his flight. He became so engrossed in something he was reading, he did not notice all the people around him had boarded the airplane. They must have called his name over the PA system, but he did not hear that either. He didn't notice anything. When he finished reading, he looked up, and he was sitting alone at the gate. Whatever he was reading must have been very interesting.

The Difference Between How You Behave at Work and at Home:

When working with groups, a comment I often hear is something like this: "I can't believe Joe is an Introvert. The way he acts in the office, I would never have guessed." My answer is, "Have you ever seen Joe at his home on the weekend?" The answer is usually no. So what the colleagues have seen is not the way Joe *is*, but the way he *behaves* in the workplace. You can learn to appear extraverted at work, but that is not the same thing as becoming an Extravert.

When people are working, it's quite common for them to be required to engage in extraverted activities. They might have to meet with clients, customers, suppliers, government officials, or confer with colleagues. They may be required to attend trade shows, conventions or other public events;

they might have to make presentations or give speeches. You can become quite skilled at these tasks, but it is not the same as *becoming* an extravert. It's a learned skill, like playing the piano, cooking, or doing math problems. You may be an expert at "working the room" during the ice breaker social hour, but this is not the same as *becoming* an extroverted type; once again, the best way to tell the difference is the effort it takes to do these tasks.

That means that performers are not necessarily Extraverts. Many are Introverts, but the real person is safe inside. They are just pretending to be someone else when they act in a play. They might have their cello in front of them in an orchestra and the audience is far away, in the dark. It's not really them out on stage.

Now, introverted types do go to parties, events, and out with friends. The difference is they usually want to be with people they know and are comfortable with, or at least with whom they have something in common. For example, if you love cats, you might have a great time at the cat show, even though there are hundreds of strangers there. That's because you have something in common with all the other participants. On the other hand, if you're at a convention for nuclear engineers, you might leave within the first five minutes because you have nothing to talk about with that group.

Can you now decide which style fits you better? After reading all of the above situations, you should have enough evidence for one side or the other. Yes, you use both sides of the scale, but which describes you *better*? In my experience, if you've read all of them and still cannot decide, an answer is not coming.

But don't be discouraged, there's no law or rule that you must be either an Extravert or an Introvert. Again, we are looking for tendencies, which side is easier for you, which side feels better. Yes, you probably do both all the time. You might be skilled in both styles, but which feels better, more comfortable, or faster to you? That's what we're trying to find out here. Again, think about the way you are at home and not what you might have learned to do for work or school.

In my experience, in almost every case in which this scale causes confusion involves an introverted type who thinks she might be an extravert; it's rarely an extraverted type who believes she might be an introvert. Why? Our society seems to prefer those who are extraverted; therefore, many introverted types learn how to act like, seem like, or pretend to be Extraverts to fit in, get along, and have success. One woman told me she consciously decided to pretend to be an Extravert when she was 11 so she would have more friends. I find it very interesting that a young girl could size up her social situation so astutely, and then come up with a plan to overcome obstacles. Of course, there's nothing wrong with being an introverted type, but this women decided she wanted different results, so she changed her behavior. She did not become an Extravert; she just learned to appear extraverted.

As I mentioned previously, if you cannot decide, you can use the letter "x", describing yourself as xSTJ, for example (Undecided, Sensing, Thinking, Judging). There are additional elements that may help you to fine-tune what you know about your personality. When people are undecided, you will often see this reflected in their results on the MBTI Step II©, which takes the four main scales and breaks them down into five facet scales, or subscales, for a total of 20 scales. There are three possibilities: in-preference, out-of-preference, or mid-zone. In-preference means it matches the style seen in the Step I results. So if you came in on the Introversion side on the Step I, and your facet scales are also on that side, they would be in-preference. If those facet scales were on the opposite side (Extraversion in this example), they would be out-of-preference. The mid-zone means either both or neither of the above. Someone who is undecided on the E-I scale will often have two facet scales on the Extravert side, two mid-zone, and one on the Introvert side, or something similar. If you would like to take the MBTI Step II, you can do so here:

http://www.discoveryourpersonality.com/
myersbriggsstepIIlongversion.html

How to Decide If You're a Sensor (S) or an Intuitive (N)

Take 30 seconds to look at these three names and write down what you notice about them; we'll discuss them later on:

Chris Storm

Lee Hart

Pat McCoy

As I said before, you probably do both Sensing and Intuitive-like activities all the time, so it's not a question of either/or. Once again, we're trying to find out which is easier for you. The Sensing style is dominant in society, and everyone has to do Sensing activities every day. Examples include eating, taking a shower, getting dressed, brushing your teeth, driving a car, etc.

In my experience, this is the scale with which people can have the hardest time. However, even those who cannot decide for themselves will often say things like, "My husband is definitely a Sensor." That means it's often easier to see which style fits another person, but your own can be more difficult. Of course, this does not mean you must be exact about your preference; it may be for both styles or neither one of them.

What Do Sensing (S) Types Like?

Sensing types are frequently very practical, down-to-earth, realistic people whose jobs involve the use of tools: dentist, electrician, farmer, welder, roofer, fire fighter, truck driver, carpenter, etc. Jobs that require paying great attention to detail are also common: accountant, auditor, surgeon, pilot, inspector, etc. When they go to college, they often study practical subjects such as engineering, nursing, or accounting because, upon graduation, they will become engineers, nurses, and accountants, all careers that require practical, down-to-earth, and realistic skills.

These can be the people who dream of one day building their own wooden boat by hand and sailing away in it or restoring an antique car to its former glory. They may spend a great deal of time working on one part of the car to get it just right. They often take great pleasure from the process of building or restoring something and can almost be sad when they are finished. They like feeling the materials they are working with, touching something that is real and has a purpose. In contrast, Intuitives are more likely to read books about sailboats or automobiles than to actually build or restore one.

Typical hobbies for Sensing types include things that involve using your hands, such as gardening, cooking, baking, handicrafts, woodworking, building things and working around the house.

The old joke is that if a Sensor loves you, she will bake you a cake. Or "nothing says lovin' like something from the oven." A woman said, "Of course, I love my children. I made them sack lunches every day for 18 years." Your Sensor might show he loves you by vacuuming the living room, painting the kitchen cabinets, or changing the oil in your truck.

Sensor Joke:

My parents came to visit me and had to change planes during the trip. My mother said, "We sat in the exact same seats on both flights." I asked her, "How did you get those seats off the first plane and onto the second plane?" A Sensor would find my very literal response quite amusing.

What Do Intuitive (N) Types Like?

Intuitive types often prefer work in which they use their heads or hearts and not their hands. They often prefer ideas, design, strategies, concepts, and the future. A good example is an architect. Architects design buildings based on their ideas, but they don't actually build anything; bringing those designs to reality depends on Sensors. The Sensors build things. They're the steelworkers, carpenters, or masons who turn ideas into reality, but they do not design buildings. Advertising is another profession where Intuitives are more likely to be found. We have marketing campaigns with talking animals, such as a duck or a green gecko, for example. It's unlikely a Sensor would come up with that idea because they know ducks and geckos can't talk. That's a fact.

Other jobs that appeal more to Intuitives include psychologist, because you can't touch fear or anxiety, or the clergy, because you can't touch God or the soul. Jobs that involve strategy, the "big picture" or design are often more appealing to Intuitives than to Sensors.

When Intuitives go to college, they frequently study things that are not "practical," such as Russian literature, art history, or anthropology. I'd guess most sociology, communications, and women's studies majors prefer Intuition as well.

Typical hobbies for Intuitive types include things such as chess (strategy), astronomy (not hands-on), fantasy games (ideas), and surfing the Internet (endless supply of ideas).

If an Intuitive loves you, he's likely to write you a love letter or a poem, or compose a song for you. They might do something dramatic and bold, like having an airplane skywrite, "Jane, will you marry me?" while you're at the beach, or have the scoreboard at a sports event flash the same message. However, you probably shouldn't expect them to polish your shoes, do your tax return, or take out the garbage.

Planning vs Execution:

Let's say we wanted to improve fire protection in a large city. An Intuitive type might analyze the data for the last five years to see where and when fires took place so fire stations, equipment, and personnel could be better located to reduce response times. They might discover Saturday nights are the worst times for fires, so they'd have more people working then. The Intuitive would come up with the plan to allocate all these resources, but here's the key difference: she wouldn't actually put out any fires herself. The firefighters on the trucks with the hoses and equipment will likely be Sensors.

Strategy vs Execution:

Another example: the amount of oil in the ground is fixed, since no more oil is being created. The people at think tanks might study global oil production and trends to see if we could answer questions such as "What is the best use of the oil we've found so far? Should we burn it as fuel or make into plastics? Can we extract more oil per hole, so we can maximize the return on investment every time we drill? Is there a better way to find and extract oil than we are currently doing?" All these things are the kinds of questions Intuitive types are likely to ponder and work on answering. However, the people on the oil rigs who are drilling the holes are more likely to be Sensors.

Creative Work vs Practical Work:

If I ask Intuitives to write a three page story about what it would be like if they were trees, most say something like this: "That's sounds like fun. I could do that. Let me think about what kind of tree I'd like to be."[5] Sensors say

---

5   One Intuitive said to me, "Three pages? I could easily write ten!" I've never heard a Sensing type say that.

something like this: "I am not and never will be a tree, so why should I waste my time doing something that dumb?"

In contrast, if a Sensor who is planning to become a radiologist is told she must memorize all 206 bones in the human body, there's usually no complaining or arguing. That's practical information she will use daily in her profession. While it's not a fun, glamorous, or exciting assignment, it is necessary, so she will get down to work memorizing bones. Intuitives will often groan about the drudgery of it all and ask why they just can't look up any bones they don't know on the Internet.[6]

Discussing "Big" Ideas:

If I ask an Intuitive, "Is there such a thing as true love?", we can often have a two hour conversation. If I ask a Sensor, the answer is, "Yes. Next question." If I ask, "What happens when we die?", it can be a long discussion with Intuitives, while Sensors say: "No one has ever come back from the dead and told us what happens, so we don't know. Next question."

Concepts vs Practical Applications:

I read that scientists have discovered the color of the universe is beige. Many Intuitives find that fascinating. When you look up at night, the sky is black, so how did they figure out it's really beige? Many Sensors say something like this: "You must be joking. That's the most useless fact I've ever heard. Are we wasting government money on

---

6   Sensors will reply that you can't spend your entire work day looking for information online. You need to know your subject well enough to function without having to check the Internet every two minutes.

junk research like this? If you want to research something practical, like drugs to treat diseases or ways to improve car safety, I can understand that. But who cares about the color of the universe?"

The Three Names Situation:

Let's go back to those three names. Here they are again:

Chris Storm

Lee Hart

Pat McCoy

These names were in an ad I saw for careers you can learn at home. When I show them to groups, the Sensing types typically focus on all the details, like pointing out the font styles, the logo colors, the italics, the phone numbers, and the ad layout. Some will notice that all the first names have one syllable. They will think about thunderstorms or snowstorms, and sometimes count the letters in all the names.

However, in less than five seconds, at least one Intuitive will say, "These are all unisex first names. They could be either men or women."[7] Yes, this ad was cleverly designed to appeal to anyone who might want to learn a new career. I can give Sensors all the time in the world and they almost never come up with that answer. However, it jumps out at the Intuitive types almost immediately. That is why we say

---

7   Yes, this is a culturally biased question. If you did not grow up in North America, you might not know that these first names are used by both men and women. For that reason, I do not ask everyone this question, but I put it in here because the principle behind the thought process is universal.

the Sensors usually see the trees, while the Intuitives often see the forest.

The Hot Air Balloon Problem:

Here's another scenario: We have a hot air balloon drifting along. The balloon is heading toward a thunderstorm and needs to rise above the storm to get to safety. The passengers have already thrown out all the sandbags, so to lose weight and go higher, someone in the balloon must jump out to save the others. In the balloon, we have three people: a heart surgeon, a chemist who is working on a fertilizer that could eliminate world hunger, and a nun who runs an orphanage. Which of these three should jump out of the balloon? The nun, the chemist or the surgeon? Take 30 seconds to come up with your answer. What was your reason for picking that person?

If you're like most people, you picked the nun. I'd guess close to 90% pick her, so don't feel bad or think you're going to hell for making that choice. Many say something like she knows she's going to heaven, or she's probably a self-sacrificing kind of person anyway so she won't mind. Others say she doesn't contribute as much to society as the others, or that she will be easier to replace. The chemist was picked about 100% of the time until I added in world hunger. Suddenly, his death rate went way down and is now the lowest of the three. When he is chosen, people will say others can look at his notes and continue his research, so we don't actually need him to finish the job. The heart surgeon is in second place, with about 9% choosing her; those who do say something like she only helps rich people who got into trouble by eating, drinking, and smoking too much. The other two help the poor and downtrodden or will make a bigger difference in the world.

The interesting thing here is the preceding paragraph is all about how Intuitives make this decision. It's about personal value, contribution to society, whose loss would be felt by more people, or who would be hardest to replace. Our friends the Sensors are smirking the whole time. The answer to this question is simple and plain as day: the heaviest person has to jump. This is a physics problem, not a moral one.

I've asked thousands of people this question. Only twice did an Intuitive come up with the correct answer. One was a helicopter pilot who asked me how much they weighed. Obviously, his work had trained him to think in terms of flying and payload. The second was a research scientist and both were INTPs. All the rest were clueless. It's fun to watch a group of Intuitives get into a long discussion on the merits of each passenger, then observe their faces when they hear the answer. They usually look quite sheepish. The point here is they almost never think in that direction. Once they hear the answer, it's obvious, but they don't come up with it on their own. The same is true for Sensors in the previous example; once they are told they are unisex names, the answer is clear. But did you see it before I told you the answer?

Different Job Levels:

Many lower level jobs involve Sensing-type activities while higher level jobs involve more Intuitive activities.

An accountant is a Sensor job, focusing on details. A Chief Financial Officer has an Intuitive job, worrying about things like a five year plan, expanding into China, investment strategies, projecting cash flow for the next year, and similar issues. The President of the United States is an Intuitive job. The president does not read thousands of job applications or conduct thousands of interviews to fill specific job openings; the president works on policies, plans and strategies to increase employment in the entire country.

Notice that I did not say you must be an Intuitive type to be a CFO, or that the President of the United States is an Intuitive type. I said these are the types of work that commonly require intuitive skills, but it does not mean you must be an Intuitive type to be in that job.

Being Creative:

Both types can be creative, but in different ways. A Sensor might say something like this: "What if we took a hammer, lengthened the handle by 1 inch, and increased the head weight by 3 ounces. We could increase the force per strike by 25%, so you'd only have to hit the nail 3 times instead of 4 to drive it into the wood." The Intuitive might ask, "Why do we need a hammer at all? Why can't we shoot nails out of a gun?" However, once the nail gun exists, it's going to be the Sensors who figure out how much it should weigh, the best spot for the handle, how much pressure is needed to fire the nails, how to load the nails for best use, etc. While the Intuitives can come up with something completely new, the Sensors usually prefer improving upon an existing idea and we often need them to make that idea a practical reality.

Preference for Sensors:

In America, Sensors make up somewhere around 75% of the population. They are the dominant group. We like them better. We say things like, "Mary has her feet on the ground," and mean it as a compliment. On the other hand, we might say, "Joe has his head in the clouds;" that is usually not a compliment, but is the way some people describe Intuitives. As a matter of fact, many Intuitives report figuring out they were different from other children at a young age, maybe 10 or 11 years old. People say things like "they march to a different drummer," or "they see the world in colors," or "they have a different way of approaching problems." Intuitives often like being "different" or "special." They often think being like everyone else would be boring.

After all these examples, you should have enough information to decide which side of the scale fits you better. If not, my experience has been that no number of additional examples will make it clear for you. That's okay. A certain percentage of people will remain undecided no matter what.

So What If You're *Still* Undecided?

If you're not sure if you're an Intuitive or a Sensor, the chances are good that you prefer Intuition. There are several reasons for this: our society prefers Sensors, every job involves some detailed work, and most people do Sensing tasks every day. That means that even if you're actually an

Intuitive, you may be functioning as a Sensor a good part of time, a fact that may obscure your actual preference. And, of course, you can utilize both.

Here's an example of using both styles: making dinner, which is clearly a Sensing task. It's real. You touch the food, chop it up, cook and eat it. However, before you can do that, you have to use some Intuition and think into the future or there will be no food in the house to cook. It might have been last week at the grocery store or in the car on the way home from work, but you have to plan ahead to make dinner. Even if it's just five minutes before dinner, you have to think into the future about what you'd like to eat.

We are looking at trends or tendencies here, not absolutes. We're looking for what is easier, what you prefer or like best, especially at home, and not what you're required to do for work. Remember, if you have to work at something, concentrate on something, or force yourself to do something, it's probably not your natural style. I'd assume some U.S. Presidents have been Sensors. Some accountants are Intuitives. There are psychologists who are Sensors and Intuitive fire fighters, and so forth. If you are a Sensor and an architect, you do not have to switch careers. None of the above predicts ability, skills, job satisfaction, success or dedication. You have free will and can choose to do whatever you like.

As I wrote in the Extravert and Introvert section, if you take the Step II test, you will probably find combinations on the five facet scales for Sensing and Intuition if you're one of the undecided. And, of course, once again, there is no rule that says you must be either a Sensor or an Intuitive, so some people use the letter "x" to mean undecided, and you could be an IxFJ (**I**ntrovert, **U**ndecided, **F**eeling, **J**udging), for example.

How to Decide If You're a Thinker (T) or a Feeler (F)

This scale describes how people make decisions. Like the other three scales, you probably use both sides of the scale every day. This scale is different from the other three because of the gender component. We'll get to that part in a bit.

What do the Thinking (T) Types Like?

People who prefer Thinking often use logic, analysis, data and numbers to make decisions. Good examples of professions that are common for them include accountants, engineers, computer specialists, and scientists. "Numbers don't lie" is a statement you might hear from Thinkers. Most businesses are run by Thinking types. They ask questions like, "How much does it cost? How long will it take? What's the bottom line?" Computers are Thinker heaven: computers don't get mad, sad, lonely, or tired. They either work or they don't. If they don't work, it's a technical problem, which we can fix. You don't have to be nice or friendly to your computer for it to function; no matter what, it will execute code the way it was programmed.

In a typical corporation, you'll likely find the Thinker types in Accounting and IT. In school, students who say they like mathematics and the sciences often prefer the Thinking style.

What do the Feeling (F) Types Like?

Feeling types tend to focus on the people (or animals) side of the equation, not numbers, money, or things. An example of a Feeler occupation is an elementary school teacher, whose job is to teach the children to read and write, not to make money for the school. A nurse's job is to help patients recover and get well, not to maximize profits for the hospital. The clergy's job is to save souls, not to increase sales income.

Whenever people say they're looking for "passion" in their jobs, it's more likely they are Feeling types. The Thinking types are more likely to ask the question, "How much does the job pay?" After all, passion does not pay the bills. Money pays the bills. There's an old joke about "any type can love you, but it takes a Feeler to really hate you." They are more likely to have intense emotions, both positive and negative.

In a typical corporation, you'll probably find the Feeler types in human resources and in marketing, particularly if the company is marketing to consumers. Jobs with the words "counselor," "therapist," "trainer," or "coach" in the title will likely appeal more to the Feeler types because of their focus on helping people. In school, Feeling types will often say they don't like mathematics at all and prefer languages, reading and writing, or the arts.

Using Feeling to Sell Products to Consumers:

Have you ever noticed what happens to the man in a shaving commercial on TV when he's finished shaving? First of all, you will observe that he is young, incredibly handsome, and doesn't actually need to shave. When he's finished, he smiles at himself in the mirror and then a beautiful young woman appears next to him, stroking his face, a woman who is clearly not his mother. I have shaved many times, yet this has never happened to me. What are we telling men with this ad? "If you shave with our product, beautiful women will be attracted to and touch you." That's not realistic, but it will give men a reason to buy specific shaving products.

What about sports car commercials on TV? The sports car is never stuck in a traffic jam on the freeway. No, that would be too realistic. Instead, the car is alone (no competing cars to distract you), speeding along the coast, through the mountains, or in the desert. Driving that car is our good-looking man again, accompanied by the beautiful woman. What are we selling you here? It's not a car. We're selling you power, independence, success, and sex appeal. If we were doing a technical sale, we'd tell you how much the car weighs, the turning radius, the cost to operate per mile and the trade-in value after five years, but no one buys a sports car because of its great turning radius.

My final example is women's shampoo commercials which, you may have noticed, never feature a woman cleaning a toilet or changing a baby's diaper. No, she is getting out of a limousine wearing a cocktail dress, going to a party or major event. She swishes her hair left and right. It is shiny and just perfect. Our good-looking man is wearing a tuxedo and taking her hand. You just know she is going to have a good time tonight. As a woman pointed out, not only will that shampoo make your hair look good, it will also make you young, thin, and beautiful, just like the woman on TV.

Interestingly, I have used these examples for people around the world. They report the same tactics are used in their own country, so it would appear the strategies of appealing to emotions work just about everywhere.

In contrast to these consumer ads, I use a technical sale. Let's say you were trying to sell jet engines to an airplane manufacturer. They won't really care about attractive human models in your ads. What they'll want to know are the specifications, such as how much the engine weighs, its fuel consumption, its power output, life expectancy, maintenance requirements, and costs. You will be using the Thinking style for this kind of transaction.

Difference in Genders for Thinking (T) and Feeling (F):

This scale is different from the other three in that in North America, we expect and want men to be Thinker types and women to be Feeler types. This is in fact true; more men are Thinker types and more women are Feeler types. That makes this scale especially tricky if you prefer the opposite side.

Women Who Prefer Thinking:

For example, women who are Thinkers are often accused of being too harsh, too bossy, too assertive, too aggressive, unfeminine, and worse – particularly by other women. Many do not fit the female stereotypes and do not especially care about their clothing, shoes, hair, makeup, jewelry, or handbag. This does not mean they pay no attention to their appearance or dress poorly. No, they often will wear what's required by the job or the occasion, because, like it or not, they know women are evaluated on their appearance; in many jobs, if you don't wear makeup to work, people will treat your poorly. But they will rarely get super excited about buying a new lipstick or getting a manicure.

Likewise, many will report it's easier to work with men than with other women. They will often complain that other women are too emotional and make no sense. And then there's the dreaded baby shower.

Many Thinker women would rather have open heart surgery in the middle of January on a busy highway with no anesthesia and a rusty butter knife than go to a baby shower. However, they cannot say that, or they will have no female friends at work. No, they have to go to the shower and pretend to have fun, play silly games, and drink that lousy punch. Meanwhile, they are thinking, "Why are we oohing and aahing? It's just a stupid t-shirt that's going to be covered with spit and baby food in a few months. It's not as if the kid won the Nobel Prize in Physics. Now that's something we could applaud!" Once again, were they to say that aloud, they'd be a pariah among the women at work.

One pregnant Thinker women asked me what she should do, since her colleagues were planning a baby shower for her and she wanted to skip it. I told her she really had no choice: she had to go and "make nice" to maintain cordial relations with her female colleagues. It's just an hour or so, so put on your happy face and pretend you're having fun. I appealed to her sense of efficiency: an ounce of prevention is worth a pound of cure. It's a lot easier to put up with a party for an hour or so than to spend months repairing relationships.

Men Who Prefer Feeling:

Men who are Feelers often have the opposite problem. They might be accused of being soft, wimpy, weak, or other negatives. Statistics vary, but it seems a great number of American men, perhaps more than 40%, are Feeler types. They usually are very good at not showing it. We generally don't like men who cry at sad movies. Sure, you can cry when your mom dies, or if your best friend gets killed next to you in battle. But a "real" man cannot cry when watching some tear-jerker movie on TV. They can't admit to being confused, scared, unsure, or nervous, particularly at work. Nope, they have to have everything under control all the time.

If a boy tells his parents that he wants to be a nurse when he grows up, I'm guessing most parents will encourage him to be a doctor instead. If he says he wants to be a secretary, I'm pretty sure he'll be going to therapy. They will also be displeased if he says he wants to be a kindergarten teacher. In contrast, I'd guess there's near-universal joy among parents if a child says he or she wants to be a brain surgeon.

The male version of the baby shower is sports. When you come into work the Monday after the Super Bowl, you better have something to say about it. If you say you missed the game because you were writing poetry, I'm guessing most of the guys in the office won't want to spend time with you anymore. Yes, you can miss the game because you had to work, take your son to the hospital, go to a funeral, or some other "valid" reason, but not liking sports relegates you to a different group of men. Now, to be clear, if you don't like sports, that doesn't mean you must be a Feeler; there are certainly plenty of Thinker types who don't like sports and plenty of Feeler men who love sports. As a matter of fact, I've found that it's common for Feeler men to like blood sports, like kickboxing or mixed martial arts. Perhaps they are overcompensating.

The Girl and the Operation Scenario:

When people cannot decide if the Feeler or Thinker style fits them better, I give them this scenario, which is based on a true story. We have a young child, around eight years old, a charity case, who comes to the U.S. from Central America for organ transplants, heart and lungs. The operation is performed, but by some mistake, she's given organs with the wrong blood type. Her body rejects them and she's connected to expensive life support equipment to keep her alive. Since she is so critically ill, she's right back up at the top of the organ recipient list. Within a week or so, the hospital receives another rare donated set of heart and lungs for the young girl. They transplant a second time, and the girl dies. She is buried with the second set of donated organs inside her.

In this scenario, the typical Thinker would say, "This girl has almost no chance of making it through the second operation alive. It's a waste of rare and valuable organs to give them to her. We should let her go, and give the organs to someone else instead." The typical Feeler will often say something like this: "It's our fault. We messed up. We have to do everything humanly possible to save this girl. We need to give her a second chance, so let's give her the second set of organs. We have to try."

What would you do? Would you give this young girl the second set of organs or not? Make an instant decision here; do not think about it. Yes or no?

As I wrote above, most Thinker types say no and most Feeler types say yes. Now we move on the second phase of our scenario. Let's say we had a test that showed the girl has only a 10% chance of surviving the second operation. However, the second child on the waiting list has an 80% chance of survival, but might die if he doesn't get donated organs in time. To which child would you give the organs now, the 10% or 80% case?

Once again, you have to make an instant decision. Who would get the organs, the first or second child?

In the second phase of our scenario, almost everyone says the 80% child should get the organs. However, there have been a few people who chose the first child no matter what. As I recall, they were all Feelers. But the vast majority of people, Thinkers and Feelers alike, choose the child with the better odds of survival. It's hard to argue with overwhelming math. Then we go on to the third phase of our scenario.

Okay, if we're going to give the organs to another child, there's no reason to keep the first child alive anymore. After all, she is a charity case, and is costing our hospital tens of thousands of dollars a day, money we'll never get back. Someone has to go into her room, turn off all the machines, and kill the girl. When you're finished, you have to tell her crying mother, who is sitting next to her daughter's bed, what you just did and why. Are you ready to go do that?

Make an instant decision: could you walk into that room and kill the girl? Yes or no?

How people react to the final phase of the scenario is fascinating. Almost everyone hesitates before answering, with Feelers taking much longer to respond than Thinker types. Most Feelers refuse to do it. They try to squirm out of it, or come up with other options: "Can someone else do it? Maybe we'll get new organs in next week we can give to her. Can we find another hospital who can take over her care?" In general, they balk at taking action. You will note that I specifically wrote "kill the girl" twice. There's a reason for this. Most Feelers react as if someone had punched them in the stomach when they hear the words, "kill the girl." Who in his right mind would want to kill a helpless, sick, young girl? I say this to people to force them into an emotional reaction. I don't want them to think about it for too long. Feelers generally have a strong reaction to the last part of our scenario and can become upset at the thought. When I push them hard enough, some will eventually agree to go into the room and end it, but it takes pressure.

Another interesting point is that when Feeler types are hesitant about what to do, I often bring up how much this charity case is costing our hospital. Invariably, this makes no difference to them. This is another key difference between the types. Thinker types can take the money into consideration, even though it's usually not the prime factor, just one of many. But Feelers will dismiss it immediately as not being part of the equation. One man, who was clearly a Thinker, interrupted me while I was describing the scenario above. He asked, "Who is paying for all of this? I'm opposed to charity cases." I've never heard a Feeling type mention that.

When a person immediately says, "Yes, I could do that," it's almost always a Thinking type. They do not take the bait I throw out about "kill the girl." They say things like, "I am not killing the girl. The operation killed the girl. She was already dead on the operating table, and only appears to be alive because she is connected to all these machines. I'm just turning off the machines and letting her go." They will say things like it's their responsibility to take action, so they will do it because it's necessary and they don't want someone else to have to do it.

To be clear, no one is happy the girl died; everyone agrees it's a tragedy. The difference in personalities is how they respond to the steps in the scenario.

I have found the above scenario particularly useful when working with men who are not sure whether they prefer Thinking or Feeling.[8] The reason is many jobs

8   When asked if he could kill the girl, one man yelled at me, "What kind of monster do you think I am?!" Yes, he was definitely a Feeler type.

require everyone, man or woman, to spend a lot of time in Thinking-type activities, so people can get confused as to what they actually prefer and what they have learned to do for work. Again, if you're not sure, the way you are at home is most likely closer to your true self than what you are required to do for work. And for most men, if they're not sure, they are more likely to be Feeling types than Thinking types, primarily because of the social pressure to fit a male stereotype. The opposite is true for women: if you can't decide, the chances are good that you prefer Thinking, as we put social pressure on women to act or behave like Feeling types.

To repeat: there is no rule or law that states you must be either a Thinker or Feeler. As before, you can decide to remain undecided. Some people use the letter "x" to indicate that choice, as in ESxJ (**E**xtravert, **S**ensing, **U**ndecided, **J**udging). That's perfectly acceptable. Yes, you likely use both sides of the scale every day. It's not a question of either/or. Yes, Thinking types cry at sad movies. Yes, Feeling types can be good at mathematics. As a matter of fact, I've spoken to a Feeling type who has a PhD. in mathematics. We are trying to figure out what is easier for you to do, what you prefer, particularly when you're not at work. The undecided will usually discover they have mixing on the Step II Thinking and Feeling facet scales.

How to Decide If You're a Judger (J) or a Perceiver (P)

Many people find this scale relatively easy. As with all the other scales, you probably do both Judging and Perceiving types of activities every day. We're trying to find out which is easier. Remember, what you do at home is more likely to be an accurate picture of your preferences than what you have learned to do for work or school. You might be tired of reading these lines, but this is so important, I want to make sure people understand it, no matter where they start reading this book. Once again, I'll provide a number of examples of both styles so you can choose which describes you better.

Notice that this scale is not called "Judgmental or Perceptive," which are common misunderstandings. This is really the lifestyle scale – how do you like to live?

What do the Judging (J) Types Like?

People who like this side of the scale better tend to be organized, neat, and like schedules and making lists. They often prefer to follow established procedures, honor traditions, and adhere to policies the organization has established. Many of them have organized their clothes closet according to a system. It might be by color, designer, season, material, short/long sleeve, pants/jackets/sweaters, etc. One man told me all the hangers in his closet are the same color, they all face the same direction, and he puts one finger between each hanger to keep them equally spaced apart. Another man told me he prepares his clothes for the coming workweek on Sunday evening. He has five hangers. He puts complete outfits for each day on one hanger: pants, shirt, socks, underwear, shoes, belt, tie, everything. When he gets up in the morning, he can take out any of the five hangers and go into the bathroom, because he had everything he needs to get dressed. Many Judging types admire and respect him for his organizational abilities, even if they don't do the same thing.[9]

If you remember the cliché of the man with a peg board for his tools with the traced outlined where each piece fits, you're thinking of the Judging style. I often joke that one of the best presents you can give a Judger is either two weeks' vacation in Hawaii or a label maker. Several people have said they love their label makers so much, they made labels that say "label maker" to put on the label makers.

---

9   In contrast, many Perceiver types find this person too organized, a bit creepy, and certainly not someone they would like to travel with for two weeks. However, one Perceiver said he would enjoy a trip with this person, because he or she would organize everything perfectly.

Another said he had to give up his label maker because he was spending too much money on labels. Apparently, he had labeled every item in his house several times.

Jobs that appeal to many Judging types include those with many rules or established procedures. A classic example is accounting. You don't create your own accounting system; there's already one that is well-established. You learn the existing rules: credits go on the right, debits on the left. Another is the military, which is Judger heaven. They have rules for everything: how to cut your hair, what color socks to wear, how to roll the sleeves up on your shirt, among many others. An electrician is another example. We have an electrical code that determines which color wire is used for which purpose. If all electricians did not follow the same code, very bad things could happen. You, as an electrician, do not get to decide on the color scheme. You will be taught the same system, no matter where you learn your trade.

Faulty Scientist:

There's an old joke that the letter "J" in personality types actually stands for "jump to conclusions." My wife is a Judging type. One day we were in a parking lot next to the parking spot for handicapped people. A young man in a sports car drove into that spot. He had long hair, loud music playing, a lot of tattoos, and looked pretty unsavory. My wife started to complain about how young people today have no respect and this lazy young man should not park in that spot, and so on. Well, when the man got out of his car, we noticed he had a prosthetic leg from his left knee down. Upon seeing this, my wife said, "Well, he shouldn't be driving so fast through the parking lot."

What happened here? This is sometimes described as "faulty scientist." That means you see the correct data, but draw the wrong conclusion. My wife saw a young man who appeared to have a complete body. That is a reasonable assumption for a 20 yr. old man; I'd guess more than 99% of young men driving cars have two whole legs. However, she didn't *know* he had two whole legs; she *assumed* (unconsciously) that he did. Yet even when she saw that he was disabled, she did not admit to jumping to conclusions. No, she found something else he did wrong.

Judging types are frequently described as "Often wrong, but never in doubt." They are convinced everyone else is wrong, and if everyone just did what they said, things would work a lot better around here. There's also an old military expression that can be applied to many Judgers, "making great time marching in the wrong direction."

Using Absolutes:

There is a tendency for many Judgers to use absolutes such as *always, never, everyone, no one*, etc. in their speech. They might not be aware of how often they say those things. When you question them closely, you will likely discover they are using these words to add emphasis to their points but what they don't realize is how they are distorting the information they're sending. Many times, what may merely be their opinion is stated like a fact.

For example, if I tell an ISFJ (**I**ntrovert, **S**ensing, **F**eeling, **J**udging) their type rarely becomes a CEO or senior executive in a corporation, they often translate that into, "He said I will never be a CEO." No, that's not what I said. I said it was rare, but as I pointed out before, there's no way to know if you're part of the 99% who won't become CEOs or the 1% who will.[10]

Similarly, Judging types can say things like, "You never tell me you love me." Translation: "You don't tell me you love me as often as I want." Or, "You never take out the garbage." Translation: "I want you to take out the garbage without my asking you to do it."

In contrast, you will notice throughout this book, I use words like *many*, *often*, *most*, *frequently*, etc., which are far from absolute. However, oddly enough, they can be transformed in the Judger's brain to *always*, *everyone*, *never*, etc. Paradoxically, for many Judging types, words like *often*, *most*, *many*, etc. can seem like "weasel words," or trying to avoid certainty. In fact, those words can be more accurate than words like *always*, *everyone*, or *never*. For example, saying *everyone* who likes chocolate ice cream also likes chocolate cake is most certainly not true. There must be at least one person on the planet who likes one but not the other. Therefore, if we say *most* people who like ice cream also like cake, we are actually being more accurate.

One comment I make to Judging types is that "different is not the same as wrong." Sure, in my examples of electrical wiring, different is wrong. For airplanes, 100% success in

---

10   Just making up numbers here. I don't know actual figures.

safe take-offs and landings is the only acceptable standard. The same is true for delivering babies: 100% success is the only acceptable standard. However, many more things in life are not that clear or crucial. Here's an example of this phenomenon:

The "Right" Way to Do Something:

A woman told a story about her brother and his family visiting her for a week or so. After a few days, her sister-in-law asked if she could help out and wash a load of towels. Sure, no problem. After she dried the towels, the sister-in-law started to fold them. As this woman watched her, her hands started to twitch, because her sister-in-law was folding the towels the WRONG way. However, being a polite person, she didn't say anything. You know what happened next? Yes, after her sister-in-law walked away, this woman refolded all the towels the way she wanted them. Now, honestly, aren't there many ways to fold towels and they will still fit in the cupboard?[11] If everything has to be done your way, and no other, you're going to be a busy person, because you're going to have to do everything yourself. People won't want to help you out. That woman should have been happy her sister-in-law was pitching in, rather than worrying about whether her towel folding methods met her standards.

What You "Should" Do:

One tip: if you are dealing with a Judger type, you can hear the word "should" a lot. The government *should* do

---

11 When I ask a group this question, people will argue with me about the one correct way to fold towels – *their* way. They loudly disagree with me when I say there are other ways to fold a towel. I'm guessing most of these protestors are Judging types.

this, children *should* do that, schools *should* teach this, other parents *should* do that, leaders of all persuasions *should* do things differently, and on and on. As the old joke goes, pretty soon we'll be "shoulding" all over ourselves trying to do things the "right" way. What the Judging types are attempting to convey is how important a particular subject is to him or her. Unfortunately, what others might hear is that there is only one correct way to do things – *my* way, of course.

Getting an Early Start:

When they have assignments due at work or school, Judging types usually want to get an early start, so they can handle any unforeseen delays. The best thing is to turn in assignments early, so they can cross them off their to-do list and then relax a bit. As a matter of fact, if they do something that wasn't on their to-do list, many of them will write it down just so they can cross it off. While it might sound strange to some, the reason is they want to get credit or the sense of satisfaction from accomplishing something. The best thing about to-do lists is being able to cross something off; that feels good. So writing something you forgot to put down gives you another opportunity to cross something off the list and feel good about what you've done. There are two systems for crossing things off the list: the first is to put a single line through the middle of the item, so you can still read what it says. The second is to have a check box on the left, and put a check mark in it. Some do both. What few people will do is completely black out the item on the list, so it's unreadable. How would you get credit for your accomplishments if you can't read them?

What do the Perceiver (P) Types Like?

Perceiving types tend to like variety, new things, spontaneity, or change just for the fun of it. They're the ones who say tidy people are just too lazy to look for things. They are the ones rushing to turn in assignments 25 minutes late at school or two days late at work. They ask others where their car keys or shoes are. Perceivers are famous for something called "floor filing." That means having stacks of papers, books, magazines, or whatever else all over every flat surface in the room, as well as in piles on the floor, chairs, windowsills, etc. They say, "Don't touch my things. I know where everything is." But no one else can find anything in all of those piles.

Perceivers are often attracted to professions where there are fewer rules. An example would be advertising. As long as the ad is effective, who cares if it features a talking gecko, tree, car, or fish? The arts are another example. There's no "right" way to sing, dance, sculpt,[12] compose, write, or paint. There is no "right" way to invent something, be a marriage or guidance counselor, or respond in a crisis. Perceivers often excel at solving problems on the spot, with little advice or help from others. They are the ones who use duct tape, spit, and baling wire to get your car moving again. It won't be pretty, but it will get you home.

Procrastination:

The saying is that the "P" in personality actually stands for "procrastinate." In America, people usually have to file their tax returns by April 15. Every year, the local TV news

12   One person disagreed with me on this. She was a Judging type.

will show the post office as midnight approaches, with lines of people trying to mail in their returns before the deadline. My guess is 99.99% of those people are Perceivers because the Judgers probably finished their taxes in February then crossed it off their to-do list.

One Perceiver told the story of being in his third year at the university without having declared a major. His faculty advisor tricked him into coming to his office and, once inside, blocked the door and said, "You're not leaving here until you pick a major." So our Perceiver friend sat down and counted up all the classes he had taken so far, and then picked the two most frequent subjects as his double major: mathematics and philosophy. He could not pick one major; he had to have at least two. This is very common, as is the resistance to making a decision.

Another Perceiver said she nearly failed university because she never turned in homework. The reason was she was never finished with her research. If she had to write a paper about the history of working women in America, there was so much information, she had a difficult time deciding what to include or exclude from her work. As a result, she missed all the deadlines. Her professors told her to just submit anything, so they could give her a grade. She would protest that she was not finished, but they made her stick to a deadline or she would never have turned in anything.

One Perceiver described her basement as being filled with paintings she had started. One day she might start to paint a sunset scene. The next morning, she would start a sunrise scene, and never go back to finish the sunset picture from the day before. This went on and on. She could not remember the last time she had actually finished a picture to her satisfaction. She was never finished with a painting, as there was always something to change, add, or improve. Needless to say, she did not earn her living as a painter.

New Experiences vs Tried and True:

Imagine you walk into a restaurant and see rhinoceros on the menu. Let's assume it's not an endangered species and you are not a vegetarian. A common Perceiver response might be, "Rhinoceros! Wow! What are the odds I'll ever see rhinoceros on the menu again? Probably zero, so I'm going to order the rhinoceros just to see what it tastes like." Judging types are more likely to say, "Rhinoceros? How much? That's too much. I'm not going to waste my money on something that probably tastes like old shoes, so I will order something I know I like."

To-Do Lists and Calendars:

On the subject of to-do lists and calendars, while it's true that many Perceiver types also use them, there's a key difference: Perceivers do it because they must, while Judgers often love to do it. If you have a busy household of five people, it can be tough to manage all those schedules without a calendar or someone who takes charge. That person might be a Perceiver, but again, it's a question of something they must do to accommodate their family's reality, rather than something they do for pleasure. Another way to tell the difference is if you made lists and schedules when you were 14 years old, before you had a family and a career. Many Judging types but few Perceivers did so. For example, one Judger said she used to schedule every day of her two week vacation before she left home, even when she was a teenager; that made her happy. You rarely find a Perceiver who does that.

Meetings:

Many organizations are dominated by Judging types. They expect people to be at the 9 a.m. staff meeting at 8:59 a.m. They want to go through the agenda items 1-2-3-4-5, and make a decision on each point before moving to the next. They like people with tidy workplaces because they are accurate, reliable, thorough, and organized. They expect coworkers and subordinates to fulfill their promises and meet deadlines.

When the Perceiving types come into the meeting at 9:10 a.m. and want to talk about agenda item #11 first, Judging types tend to get upset. To begin with, there isn't even a #11 on the agenda. Then the Perceivers talk about items 3-5-4-1-2, in that order, with no decision on any point, because we need to "check into some more facts first." By this time, the Judger types will be really upset, because they've just wasted 90 minutes, have accomplished nothing, and now have 35 messages piling up they need to answer while they're stuck in the meeting making zero progress on the actual issues.

To avoid such conflicts and problems, many Perceiver types learn how to act like Judging types at work. For example, they might have a very neat work space; but take a look inside their cars, and you will see something different, i.e., a lot of junk. Let me correct that: it's not junk, it's their "stuff."

What If You *Still* Can't Decide?

If you're not sure which side you prefer, you're more likely to be a Perceiving type, particularly if there's a large gap between what you like to do at home or in your private life and what you are required or have learned to do, for work or school. If your workplace is rather neat and tidy and your living room is rather untidy, your living room is probably a better indicator of your style than the workplace.

Sure, there are Judging types who are frequently late. There are Perceiving types who love making lists. As before, we are talking about tendencies.

Again, there is no rule or law that says you must be either a Judger or Perceiver type. Yes, you probably do some of both styles, particularly at work. Most of us have to perform Judging activities every day. We have to be at work at a certain time. We may have to pick up children from day care or sports events. We might have to use public transportation. All are things that require us to adhere to a time schedule. Whether we like it or not, we have to be there on time or we'll miss the bus.

However, most of us have a preference for one side over the other, even if we are forced to do a lot of non-preferred tasks. You can remain undecided, use the letter "x" and call yourself an ISTx (**I**ntrovert, **S**ensing, **T**hinking, **U**ndecided). You can change your mind at any time. If you decide that one style fits you better six months from now, that's okay. You might find that spending more time around Perceivers will help you decide whether you are more similar to them or to Judging-types. At the end of the day, it's your decision. Again, if you take the Step II version of the MBTI, you'll probably find some mixing on the Judging and Perceiving facet scales.

At this point, we will change the discussion to address some issues that affect certain personality types more frequently than others. Let's start with Intuitive Disease.

Intuitive (N) Disease

I made up this name, but not the phenomenon it represents. This is something that many Intuitive types fall afoul of in their daily lives. It's based in part on the old joke about two psychologists passing each other in the hall. One says, "Good morning." The other thinks, "What did she mean by that?" It's also related to the line, often attributed to Freud, that sometimes "a cigar is just a cigar."

Here are three scenarios for you to think about:

Imagine I passed you in the hall one day at work, said, "Nice shoes" and kept on walking. Imagine a tone of voice that was neither clearly positive nor sarcastic. Many Intuitive types would start asking themselves: "What did he mean by that? Does he like my shoes or does he think they're odd-looking? Was that a friendly or a sarcastic smile? He's been saying a lot of strange things to me lately, so I think he was being a jerk about it." Is that really what happened?

One day, my wife and I were planning to go to the movies after dinner. During dinner she said, "I'm so tired." What's your first reaction? Do you think she still wanted to go to the movies? Most Intuitive types immediately think she does not want to go.

A client goes to see a therapist. The therapist says, "Tell me about your mother." The client says, "My mom was okay." Many Intuitive therapists would immediately think, "Aha! He doesn't like his mother." Of course, he didn't say that; what the client said was his mother was okay . . . not terrible, not great, just okay.

There are two steps to working on this problem. The first is to always assume a positive meaning; the second is to "ask the question." Let's go back to the example about "nice shoes." Do you know what most people mean when they say "nice shoes"? Surprise! They mean they like your shoes. If you always assume people are sincere when they say they like your shoes, you will probably be right 80% of the time. But, yes, there will be those people who do not like your shoes. This brings us to the second step. There is a simple way to find out what people really meant: ask them! If you're not sure, ask the question: "Do you really like my shoes?" You will get an answer. Many Intuitives refuse to ask the question and just assume the negative. That means they are probably wrong 80% of the time.

In the second example, when my wife does not want to go to the movies, she says, "I don't want to go to the movies." She does not hint at it; she just says it. If I'm not sure, I can always ask, "Do you still want to go to the movies?" and I receive a direct and certain answer.

In the third case, if you are a therapist and a client says his mother is okay, you really don't know what he means, so you have to ask the question: "I'm not sure what 'okay' means for you. Could you explain it to me in greater detail?" Let the client tell you what he meant. Don't assume you know the answer, because there's a chance you're wrong.

This tendency to assume they have heard information correctly can get Intuitive types into a lot of trouble. That's because what they believe they heard and what the speaker actually meant can be two different things. Yet many Intuitive types, as I mentioned, do not follow up with a question. Since they don't ask the question, they act upon assumptions, which can be wrong.

Perceiver (P) Disease

Don't worry, it's not fatal. I use this term to describe two common issues that Perceiver types face. The reason I call it a disease is it's unlikely to go away and there's probably no surefire cure. Perceiver disease has two parts: the first is the worry they will pick the wrong option and the second is, "Been there, done that." Let's look at these two parts in detail.

What If I Pick The Wrong Option?

When faced with two or more choices, many Perceivers are worried: "What if I pick Option 1, and Option 2 is better? What if 3 is better than 2? What if 4 is better than 3? And what about number 5?!"

Of course, you also can be very decisive. Here's my example: what would you rather do . . . take a two week vacation in Tahiti or spend ten years in prison? Of all the people I've asked, no one has ever taken more than a second to say "Tahiti." They had zero doubts they were making the correct decision. Why? Because the options are extremely different. It's clear which answer is best.

Now here's another choice: Would you prefer a two week vacation in Tahiti or in Fiji?[13] Now the Perceiver types hit the brakes. They're not sure, they need to do some research, watch some videos, check with people who have been there, read up on both places, and really think things over before making a decision. Why? Because they are quite similar. Perceivers want to be sure they're picking the right vacation, so they will spend a lot of time and energy deciding which one is "best."

Okay, let's assume you pick Fiji in the second scenario. You fly down there and it pours rain the entire two weeks. Those same two weeks, there was blazing sunshine and beautiful weather in Tahiti. Darn, you picked the wrong option! Of course, you couldn't possibly know if it was going to rain when you made your decision months earlier to go to Fiji. The future is unknowable, so you made a decision based on what you *thought* was going to be best. No amount of research and no person on the planet can tell you if it's going to be raining six months from now in Fiji.

In many situations, any choice will entail a loss. If you pick Option 1, you can't have Option 2. If you go to Tahiti, you lose the option of going to Fiji and vice versa. Even if you think you're being clever by going to Tahiti for one week and Fiji for one week, it still might rain the entire second week on Fiji and be sunny on Tahiti. And by the way, the second week in Tahiti is when the whales came

13   If you have been to either of these places, pick two spots you have not visited. How about Tonga and Vanuatu?

by, so you missed seeing them as well. Many Perceiver types are loath to make these decisions because they want a guarantee they are choosing the right option. Sorry to disappoint you, but there are no guarantees.

Again, if the best answer were clear, we wouldn't have to think about it or discuss it. We would automatically make the "right" decision, like in our prison or Tahiti example. When you're faced with decisions where the "correct" answer is uncertain or the future is unknowable, <u>it doesn't matter which option you pick</u>. Yes, you can just flip a coin, roll the dice, throw a dart at the dart board, or pick a number out of a hat. You might be shocked to hear this, but it *really* makes no difference. You can't possibly know the future, so you're wasting your time trying to figure it out. Just pick one and see what happens.

One way to make a decision is to write all your options on a piece of paper and put them in a hat. You tell yourself, "Whatever I pick out of the hat is what I'm going to do." Let's say you pick out Fiji and you get this feeling that you want to pick again. That's a clear sign you really don't want Fiji. The challenge many Perceiver types face is they will pull all the paper slips out of the hat and won't like any option. Yes, they want that clarity; they want to be sure, which they can't be.

Remember, when there is no way to be sure, then it doesn't matter which option you choose. This is the opposite of what most Perceivers do: they put lots and lots of effort into trying to be sure. It's all a waste of time. It doesn't matter. Hard to accept, but true.

Here's another way to think about it. Imagine you have 60 seconds to make a decision: you will have to choose one food that will be the only thing you will eat every day for the rest of your life. How would you like to make that decision? Most Perceiving-types would hate it. Let's try a different scenario: within the next 60 seconds, you will have to choose one food that will be the only thing you will eat every day for the next two months. Isn't that a much easier decision? Of course it is. Okay, let's substitute the word "career" for "food." For many people, it's much easier to pick something you want to do for the next three years than to choose something you will have to do for the next 40. By shortening your mental time frame, you'll reduce the pressure on yourself.

Been There, Done That

It's very common for Perceiver types to change their minds. Here's how I explain it: let's say you're trying to find the "right" career for you. I have a crystal ball. The correct career for you is file clerk. For the rest of your working days, you will be a file clerk. Upon hearing this news, most Perceivers get depressed and probably start thinking about ending their lives quickly, rather than enduring many years of filing.

The paradox is this: there is no "right" answer. If there were a correct answer, you wouldn't like it anyway. So you have to be *happy* you don't know what you're going to be doing 5, 10, 15, or 20 years from now. It's the old joke, "the only difference between a rut and a grave are the dimensions." Being stuck in a rut is as bad as being dead.

This is a moment of truth for many Perceivers: somewhere inside, they've been holding out hope that someone has the answer for them, the "right" career, where they'll be happy forever. In their heart of hearts, they know it's not true, but they wish it were. When confronted with the news that such a career does not exist and how wonderful it is that this is the case, they can grow despondent. However, after a few minutes of thinking about it, most are relieved. They can finally stop chasing ghosts. They can stop pressuring themselves to "figure it out," "settle down," "get their act together," and other such statements.

At this point, they often say something like this: "But all my friends have careers, families, big houses, nice cars, and exotic vacations. I want that too." Great, but are you willing to do the same things your friends did to get those things in life? The answer is usually no. Secondly, you are not your friends. You are wired differently. Those things likely won't make you happy, nor will you be able to put up with the cost of getting there long enough to make it.

Many Perceivers are going to change their minds anyway within a few weeks, months, or years, so why worry about what you're going to do? It's an impossible burden at age 20 to figure out what the rest of your life will look like. We cannot predict the next five seconds, let alone 50 years. So I tell Perceivers to think about what they'd like to do next, as opposed to the rest of their lives; whatever that is, if it turns out they don't like it, they can always do something else.

It is true you are likely to feel pressure from friends, family and society to settle down and get a career going, etc., but that's their *opinion*, not a fact. You can have 25 careers if you want. Careers, not jobs. You have to live your own life, not someone else's agenda.

Here's a story to illustrate my point. I spoke to a woman who went to Catholic school as a child. When she graduated, she became a nun, because she felt God had called to her. She became a missionary in Central America. While there, she left the church because they had too many rules and she didn't like the way women were treated. But she loved the people with whom she was working, so she stayed there for several more years to help build houses for low-income families. She got tired of that and came back to the United States and made her living singing Spanish songs in Mexican restaurants. She grew tired of that and moved to Spain to teach English and study guitar. She grew tired of that and came back to the United States and started her own management consulting company. Would you expect a nun to run a management consulting company? No. Is there a rule that says she can't? No. She lived in many different places and did many things. She did not die. She was never homeless. She's not the richest person in dollars, but she has lived a life rich in experiences. Many Perceiver types say they'd love to have lunch with her and ask her about her life, because she probably has many interesting stories to tell. In contrast, if I said this women had studied accounting, then worked as accountant, rising up to become CFO of a major corporation, few Perceivers would be interested in asking her to tell them about her life.

Intuitive – Feeler (NF) Issues

I'm guessing many of you reading this book are Intuitive Feeler types (**IN**tuitive **F**eeler). They frequently love this subject and think it's the cat's meow, the best thing since sliced bread, or canned beer. Some believe this personality theory explains the universe. They are also the types to most commonly have work-related difficulties, since so many of the professions they like are low on the pay scale or not jobs at all, like poet or blogger. (You do have a blog, don't you?)

Other issues arise for these types because many are highly idealistic, spiritual (not necessarily religious) people. Does the average corporation care if you have a soul? Nope, just how much money we earned this week. Many NF types want to make the world a better place, to make life better for people, or to make a difference. Just earning money and then dropping dead is not a real life. It's an empty life. They are often looking for meaning in life and in particular, in work. In contrast, many Sensing-Thinking (ST) types say work is work, and if you're looking for inspiration, go to church on Sunday. I say be glad you haven't found the true meaning of life, so you have a reason to get out of bed tomorrow. The journey can continue. *Climbing* the mountain is the challenge, not standing on top.

In my experience, NF types are most likely to feel insulted or disrespected by others. They are probably offended reading the previous sentence. Part of the reason is Intuitive Disease, as described above; the other is that the Feeling types tend to take remarks personally, unlike the Intuitive-Thinking (NT) types.

People-Pleasers and Conflict Avoiders

Many NF types are people pleasers and conflict avoiders. One of the standard examples I use is the cliché of the girlfriend asking her boyfriend, "What are you thinking about?" The boyfriend answers, "Nothing." She thinks to herself, "He is thinking about other women. He doesn't love me anymore. It's all over! I knew it!" What is he really thinking about? Nothing! If he says he's thinking about nothing, he's thinking about nothing. But the NF types don't believe him. They think he's lying. They don't trust him. Maybe he's thinking about buying new boot laces or changing the oil on his truck, but they still don't believe him. So off they go to ruminate in a corner someplace. They come back two hours later to yell at him for something he did not do. He wonders why she's yelling at him. He didn't do anything. She asked him a question, and he answered. What's the problem?[14]

Would You Own a Minivan?

One question I ask NF men, if they have no children, is whether they would ever drive a minivan. Generally, the answer is no; it's not "manly" enough. In my experience, they tend to be more particular about their hair, clothing, and appearance than NT men. They tend to be more worried about what others think of them, of offending people. They probably apologize more than many other people.

Intuitive – Thinker (NT) Issues

The second group most likely to be reading this book would be the NT types (INtuitive Thinking). They often fall victim to the "paralysis by analysis" I mentioned before. They think if they analyze something long enough, they will get an answer and everything will be clear. However, things like love stump them, because they defy analysis.

When people are not sure if they are NF or NT types, I give them some examples. NF types are more likely to believe in God, or some higher power. They believe we're not here by accident, that life has a purpose, even if we can't see it clearly right now. They may spend years searching for that purpose, which is actually a whole lot of fun. They might complain about not finding the answer, but, in reality, they don't want to find it because then life would be over. It's like Nirvana: you're not supposed to find it; you're supposed to look for it. "The journey is the destination" and other such sayings apply here.

In contrast, it's far more likely our NT friends will be atheists. They ask questions like why God never appears on TV or tells everyone at the same time what He wants, why is there absolutely no physical evidence God exists, or why babies get cancer. When there's a war, both sides ask God for help in vanquishing their enemies. Whose side is God on? NTs are more likely to be the young children who figure out Santa Claus cannot be real, since even if he took just 1 second per house, he could only visit 3,600 houses per hour, so in one night, he couldn't even finish Seattle. And by the way, did you look at the size of the chimney? It's 8 inches square, so how can a 300 lb. man with a sack of toys fit down there? (The NF answer: it's magic.) Santa, like God, doesn't pass the NT common sense test. Does this mean you must be an atheist if you're an NT type? Of course not, these are just examples of tendencies, not absolutes.

The NT buying a car would commonly look at the statistics: which car had the lowest cost to operate, the fewest repairs, and highest trade in value. They would then buy a two or three year old used car, so some other person would take the depreciation hit. They might buy a canary yellow car if they discovered they were the least popular, and therefore sold at the greatest discount. They would not care if it's ugly, fast, or popular. They want reliable transportation at the lowest cost per mile. They want utility, not a manifestation of their worth as a human being.

I use the cliché of the unkempt old man in his bathrobe and slippers shopping at a grocery store for two cans of cat food with a coupon for 24 cents off each can. He then gets into a 1974 Ford Pinto and drives back to his modest house. This man has $8 million in the bank and is quite likely an NT type. To him, money isn't for fancy food or a luxurious car; money means having the ability to tell everyone to go to hell without worrying about the consequences.

Paralysis by Analysis

This is a common affliction among NT types. They want to be sure they have the correct answer. Some things cannot be analyzed. Love is an example. I love chocolate. So do you. Is my love of chocolate a 5 and yours a 4? What about romantic love? Are you going to analyze your partner to make sure he or she is really the one you want? How will you measure that? What are your metrics?

What many analytical types forget is that, at some point, analysis fails. They frequently do not notice when they have crossed the line from making progress to wasting time. My example: if I put you inside a paper bag, you can analyze it for 200 years, yet you're still stuck inside. If I give you a knife, you can cut your way out in 20 seconds. Another example: researching careers on the Internet. After two hours, you probably will have found 99% of the most important information. Anything really bad or really good will show up in those two hours. Each additional hour of Internet research brings a decreasing return. Many are looking for the "knock-out punch," the one fact that will clear up any confusion and show them what the "best" answer is. Well, if you don't find it in the first hour or two, it probably doesn't exist, so now you're wasting time again. You can go crazy trying to find out the "hidden" truths or "secrets" people don't know. Well, if it's on the Internet, it's not secret. For example, if there were something that truly cured baldness in men, it would be on every major news site, all the TV networks, and all the international news outlets the same day, within hours or minutes of each other. If you find some obscure blog where someone claims to have the cure, it's not real.

Paradoxically, the more research you do, the more facts you gather, the harder it will be to make a decision. Why? Because you will find more positives and negatives on any option, and no knock-out punch, so you'll wind up like a cat chasing its tail, going in a circle. More information does not mean a better, easier, or faster decision. On the contrary, it will get you stuck in quicksand. Then you have the "paralysis by analysis" problem.

This means that action beats thinking about things every time. Mindless action is better than endless contemplation because the chances are better something positive will happen. Many NTs never get to the execution phase of their plans. Sure, they have many great ideas, but they struggle to implement them. Remember, it's what you do that counts, not what you think about. You might have a great idea for a new business, but if you never do it, what's the point? It's like the old saying, "The road to hell is paved with good intentions." Talking about plans, thinking about plans, or writing plans, while all good, are just the first step. The three most important parts are action, action, and action.

Can My Personality Type Change?

The short answer is it's difficult to know if it's possible. Sure, based on personal observation, we might think the easy answer to this question is "yes," but few things are that easy.

Many of us can think of specific examples from our own lives: "Joe was outgoing and talkative, but since his wife died, he's become withdrawn and quiet." There's no way to know if Joe was always quiet and withdrawn, but living with his wife made him outgoing and talkative. Another possibility is that Joe would have become quiet and withdrawn even if his wife hadn't died. Maybe his wife's death caused him to withdraw; he might be suffering from depression, so what we are seeing are the symptoms of an affliction and not a personality change. There's no way to know with 100% certainty if any or all of these are true.

Remember, correlation is not causation. The fact they happened at the same time does not mean Event A caused

Event B. A good example of this is people who refuse to get flu shots because the one year they did get a flu shot, they got the flu. In their minds, the flu shot caused the flu. This is not physically possible, yet people still believe it's true. There's no way to know if they would've gotten the flu anyway, or if the flu would've have been worse if they hadn't received the shot. The only thing that's 100% certain is the flu shot did not give them the flu, but good luck trying to convince them otherwise.

Another line of reasoning is people develop over time, so the things that were interesting and exciting to you at 20 might not be so thrilling at 70. For example, you might have enjoyed certain television shows, music, or computer games when you were 10 years old. It's likely you will not enjoy those things as much when you're 40 years old. So did your personality change or did you grow up?

Your life stage often influences what you focus on. In their 20s, many people are interested in completing their education, starting work or a career, and perhaps finding a life partner with whom they can have a family. In contrast, at age 70, most people will be focused on health issues and retirement. Very few will be looking to start a career, family, or college at age 70. Did your personality type change or did you grow older?

We can use the analogy of an acorn. Under the right conditions, it will become an oak tree. So was the oak tree "sleeping" inside the acorn, waiting for the right moment to come out? Did the acorn change into an oak tree, or was it always an oak tree, just in a different form? [15] If you went to a lot of parties and social events at 20 so you could meet people, but now, at age 45, you're content to spend time at home with your family, were you extraverted at age 20 and introverted at 45, or an introvert who did what was necessary to meet new people at age 20?

To truly answer the question about changing personalities, we'd have to have a fail-safe way of testing infants and old folks to see if they stayed the same or changed. My hunch is we'd find most stayed the same, but some changed. So we're back to the same old problem: will you change? No way to know. Even if we could determine that 98% of people never change, you might be part of the 2% who do.

Returning to our acorn analogy: if the young tree gets enough water, light and nutrients, it will grow a certain way. If it gets less than optimal amounts of any of them, it will grow a different way, but it will always be an oak, not a pine or apple tree. Likewise, life events will influence how each of us develops. You might lose your legs in a car accident at 18. That will certainly change how your life will proceed from there, but will it change your personality? It's impossible to know, because we are not able to compare that life to one without the car accident. You might be similar or very different. Once again, on the surface, the obvious answer is you will be a different person after the accident, but we really can't know for certain.

---

15 I put this in here for the Intuitive types, who commonly love analogies and metaphors. Sensors often scratch their heads and dismiss the whole line of reasoning. They've seen people change, so the answer is clear and we're wasting time talking about it. ☺

I should point out that the question of whether or not your personality can change is not the same as whether or not your MBTI results can change. They are two different things. You might determine that the ISFP (**I**ntrovert, **S**ensing, **F**eeling, **P**erceiving) description fits you best, but your MBTI results might come out differently each time. This means your results changed, not your personality.

Another situation can arise when people take the MBTI during major life events or transitions perhaps because, during those times, they question who they are, what they have done in the past, what the future should be like, and more. Examples of such major events include losing your job, getting divorced, retiring, the death of a loved one, graduating college, moving to a new town, getting married, having a baby, etc. It doesn't have to be a negative event. Most people would put having a baby in the positive column, but it's also true you will have major life adjustments after adding a new person to your family. Therefore, it's possible you would've gotten different results six months earlier or six months later, but right now, the results can be skewed by the changes in your life. That's not the same as changing your personality. It's being at a stage or in a phase that changes your usual approach to life. That can cause you to answer the questions differently, which could change your results.

In general, people tend to become more self-aware as they age. Often people say things like: "I used to think I was an Extravert, but now I realize I've been an Introvert all along." They might think they fit the Extravert profile when they're 20, but at 60, they often can see themselves quite clearly. They have the wisdom, experience, and self-knowledge of 60 years, which means they often are aware of how they tried to meet others' expectations at a younger age. By age 60, they frequently don't care anymore what others think about them.

How Often Should I Take the Myers-Briggs?

Sometimes people get results on the MBTI that do not fit them, or are not what they are expecting, or what they want. A common reaction is to want to take the MBTI again right away to see if the results come out "better." This rarely helps.

My experience has been that when a person says the results are off or do not fit, they are looking for a certain answer. If they take the MBTI again the next day or sooner, they tend to over-analyze the questions and become even more frustrated with the results the second time.

It's far better to speak to a counselor about your results and find out why they seem off or don't fit you. Common reasons include people thinking they "should" be a certain way, wishing they could be a certain way, their parents, friends or families tell them to be a certain way, the work vs home issue, etc.

I've also noticed that when I speak to people and give them examples of the different sides of the scales, if they cannot decide after 10 or 15 examples, they will not be able to decide after 20 or 30. There's the law of diminishing returns involved here. Most of the time, after the first five examples or so, people are either sure or they are not. But, as I said previously, there is no rule that says you have to be an Intuitive or a Sensing type. You can be both, you can be neither.

When I talk to people who have taken the MBTI, I'd guess about 75% of people don't remember their type. The longer it's been, the less likely they are to remember. (This is usually not the case with Intuitives. They tend to remember the results longer than others.)

I tell people taking the MBTI is like looking in the mirror: it should reflect back what you think and feel about yourself when you take it. If you say the results are off, it's a red flag, and means the discussion needs to focus on why.

As I mentioned earlier, be sure you're actually taking the genuine MBTI and not some imitation. The free tests can be quite inaccurate.

If you do want to take the MBTI again, I suggest waiting a good amount of time, say six months, before coming back and trying once more. That should give you enough time to think about other things instead of worrying about how accurately you answered the questions. It will also give you time to read about different personality types. You might find one type fits you better than the others after some research. If you think the ISTJ description fits you best, who cares if your MBTI came out ISFP? You're the final authority.

What If I *Still* Can't Decide What Type I Am?

If you're completely stuck, you're probably a Perceiver, first of all. It's far more likely to happen to them than Judgers, in my experience. Let's say you're stuck between ENFP (**E**xtraversion, I**N**tuition, **F**eeling, **P**erceiving) and ESFP (**E**xtraversion, **S**ensing, **F**eeling, **P**erceiving). Both describe you somewhat, but neither really grabs you as an accurate description.

My recommendation is to get the two descriptions, ENFP and ESFP, and give them to people who know you well OUTSIDE of work and ask them to pick which fits BETTER. Both will fit somewhat, that we know. But sometimes you cannot see the forest while standing among the trees. Sometimes others can see you more clearly than you can see yourself. Probably the best people to ask are your parents or the adult(s) who raised you, if possible, because they likely saw you good, bad, and ugly. They probably saw you throwing a tantrum or two, but your colleagues probably haven't. Brothers and/or sisters are good choices; you probably had a fight or two with them growing up, so they have seen you in all kinds of moods. Cousins, old school friends, your spouse or significant other, your adult children, college friends, golf buddies, anyone you spend a lot of time with, are all good people to ask.

I recommend you stay away from colleagues, former bosses, and anyone you know in a work environment. They probably haven't seen you in your "angry" state very often, if ever. While your family likely has seen you every way, your coworkers probably have seen only the nice version of you. And remember, behavior is not the same as personality because you can choose, stop, start, and modify your behavior, but you do not get to choose your personality.

Let's say you give 12 friends and family the two type descriptions and seven of them choose ENFP as the better fit. I would use that type as my working hypothesis. It's not set in stone and you can change your mind at any time but still, I'd give a lot of weight to the family's opinion. You might find, as you read more about a particular type, that one fits you better than the other. At some point, after doing all the reading and asking people for their interpretation, if you still are not sure, I'd give it a rest. It's not a life-or-death decision you must make today or, for that matter, ever. There will probably always be a certain percentage of people who will never decide, and that's okay.

_____

About the Author

Brian Jones has been offering the Myers-Briggs Type Indicator through his website, DiscoverYourPersonality. com, since 2001. Over the years, he has spoken to many thousands of people about personality types.